THIS JOURNAL BELONGS TO:

_____

_____

_____

www.prettysimplebooks.com

@prettysimplebooks

Want a freebie?!

Email us at
prettysimplebooks@gmail.com

Title the email "Gratitude!" and
we'll send you something fun!

· ·

Visit our website

www.prettysimplebooks.com

And find us on Instagram

@prettysimplebooks

grat·i·tude

noun

the feeling of being thankful; readiness to
show appreciation for and to return kindness.

• •

Are you ready to change your entire way of
thinking? I know, that sounds extreme, however,
if you use this journal and make a daily habit of
writing down just three things you are thankful
for every day, I think you will be surprised at the
change you see in yourself, your wellbeing, and
your happiness! Starting every day with some
quiet time, reflecting on the little things (or the big
things!) that you are thankful for, is a sure way to
start the day on the right note. If we constantly
focus on what we don't have, how in the world
do we expect to be happy? But if we choose to
see the blessings all around us, big or small – a
beautiful, sunny day, a good cup of coffee, that
first savory taste of your favorite dark choco-
late, the smell of rain after a storm – we begin to
focus on the good things in life, the little things
that sometimes mean the most. Take five minutes,
write down three things, just three simple things,
and remember to seek the beauty in this life that
you've been given.

• •

GOOD DAYS START WITH

GRATITUDE

Happiness cannot be traveled to, owned, earned, worn or consumed. Happiness is the spiritual experience of living every minute with love, grace, and gratitude.

– Denis Waitley

I AM THANKFUL FOR...   DATE:

1. _____
2. _____
3. _____

I AM THANKFUL FOR...   DATE:

1. _____
2. _____
3. _____

I AM THANKFUL FOR...   DATE:

1. _____
2. _____
3. _____

I AM THANKFUL FOR...   DATE:

1.
2.
3.

I AM THANKFUL FOR...   DATE:

1.
2.
3.

I AM THANKFUL FOR...   DATE:

1.
2.
3.

I AM THANKFUL FOR...   DATE:

1.
2.
3.

CULTIVATE AN ATTITUDE OF GRATITUDE.

What were the highlights of your week?

GOOD DAYS START WITH

GRATITUDE

The more you praise and celebrate your life,
the more there is in life to celebrate.

– Oprah Winfrey

I AM THANKFUL FOR...   DATE:

1. _____
2. _____
3. _____

I AM THANKFUL FOR...   DATE:

1. _____
2. _____
3. _____

I AM THANKFUL FOR...   DATE:

1. _____
2. _____
3. _____

I AM THANKFUL FOR...   DATE:

1. _____
2. _____
3. _____

I AM THANKFUL FOR...   DATE:

1. _____
2. _____
3. _____

I AM THANKFUL FOR...   DATE:

1. _____
2. _____
3. _____

I AM THANKFUL FOR...   DATE:

1. _____
2. _____
3. _____

CULTIVATE AN ATTITUDE OF GRATITUDE.

What were the highlights of your week?

GRATITUDE

I don't have to chase extraordinary moments
to find happiness – it's right in front of me if I'm
paying attention and practicing gratitude.

- Brene Brown

I AM THANKFUL FOR...　　　DATE:

1. _____
2. _____
3. _____

I AM THANKFUL FOR...　　　DATE:

1. _____
2. _____
3. _____

I AM THANKFUL FOR...　　　DATE:

1. _____
2. _____
3. _____

I AM THANKFUL FOR...   DATE:

1. _____
2. _____
3. _____

I AM THANKFUL FOR...   DATE:

1. _____
2. _____
3. _____

I AM THANKFUL FOR...   DATE:

1. _____
2. _____
3. _____

I AM THANKFUL FOR...   DATE:

1. _____
2. _____
3. _____

CULTIVATE AN ATTITUDE OF GRATITUDE.

What were the highlights of your week?

GOOD DAYS START WITH

GRATITUDE

> Shine brightly. See beauty. Speak kindly. Love truly. Give freely. Create joyfully. Live thankfully.
>
> *- Mary Davis*

I AM THANKFUL FOR...   DATE:

1. _____
2. _____
3. _____

I AM THANKFUL FOR...   DATE:

1. _____
2. _____
3. _____

I AM THANKFUL FOR...   DATE:

1. _____
2. _____
3. _____

I AM THANKFUL FOR...   DATE:

1. _____

2. _____

3. _____

I AM THANKFUL FOR...   DATE:

1. _____

2. _____

3. _____

I AM THANKFUL FOR...   DATE:

1. _____

2. _____

3. _____

I AM THANKFUL FOR...   DATE:

1. _____

2. _____

3. _____

CULTIVATE AN ATTITUDE OF GRATITUDE.

What were the highlights of your week?

GOOD DAYS START WITH

GRATITUDE

Gratitude is the healthiest of all human emotions.
The more you express gratitude for what you
have, the more likely you will have even more
to express gratitude for.

- Zig Ziglar

I AM THANKFUL FOR...   DATE:

1. _____
2. _____
3. _____

I AM THANKFUL FOR...   DATE:

1. _____
2. _____
3. _____

I AM THANKFUL FOR...   DATE:

1. _____
2. _____
3. _____

I AM THANKFUL FOR...   DATE:
. . . .
1.
2.
3.

I AM THANKFUL FOR...   DATE:
. . . .
1.
2.
3.

I AM THANKFUL FOR...   DATE:
. . . .
1.
2.
3.

I AM THANKFUL FOR...   DATE:
. . . .
1.
2.
3.

• •

CULTIVATE AN ATTITUDE OF GRATITUDE.

What were the highlights of your week?

• •

GOOD DAYS START WITH

GRATITUDE

> I like people who get excited about the change of seasons, the sound of the ocean, watching a sunset, the smell of rain, starry nights.
>
> *– Brooke Hampton*

I AM THANKFUL FOR...   DATE:

1. _____
2. _____
3. _____

I AM THANKFUL FOR...   DATE:

1. _____
2. _____
3. _____

I AM THANKFUL FOR...   DATE:

1. _____
2. _____
3. _____

I AM THANKFUL FOR...   DATE:

1. _____
2. _____
3. _____

I AM THANKFUL FOR...   DATE:

1. _____
2. _____
3. _____

I AM THANKFUL FOR...   DATE:

1. _____
2. _____
3. _____

I AM THANKFUL FOR...   DATE:

1. _____
2. _____
3. _____

CULTIVATE AN ATTITUDE OF GRATITUDE.

What were the highlights of your week?

GOOD DAYS START WITH

GRATITUDE

> When you arise in the morning, think of what a precious privilege it is to be alive - to breathe, to think, to enjoy, to love.
>
> *- Marcus Aurelius*

I AM THANKFUL FOR...   DATE:

1. _____
2. _____
3. _____

I AM THANKFUL FOR...   DATE:

1. _____
2. _____
3. _____

I AM THANKFUL FOR...   DATE:

1. _____
2. _____
3. _____

I AM THANKFUL FOR...   DATE:
· ·

1. _____

2. _____

3. _____

I AM THANKFUL FOR...   DATE:
· ·

1. _____

2. _____

3. _____

I AM THANKFUL FOR...   DATE:
· ·

1. _____

2. _____

3. _____

I AM THANKFUL FOR...   DATE:
· ·

1. _____

2. _____

3. _____

· ·

CULTIVATE AN ATTITUDE OF GRATITUDE.

What were the highlights of your week?

· ·

GOOD DAYS START WITH

GRATITUDE

> The small happy moments add up. A little bit of joy goes a long way.
>
> *- Melissa McCarthy*

I AM THANKFUL FOR...   DATE:

1. _____
2. _____
3. _____

I AM THANKFUL FOR...   DATE:

1. _____
2. _____
3. _____

I AM THANKFUL FOR...   DATE:

1. _____
2. _____
3. _____

I AM THANKFUL FOR...   DATE:

1. _____

2. _____

3. _____

I AM THANKFUL FOR...   DATE:

1. _____

2. _____

3. _____

I AM THANKFUL FOR...   DATE:

1. _____

2. _____

3. _____

I AM THANKFUL FOR...   DATE:

1. _____

2. _____

3. _____

CULTIVATE AN ATTITUDE OF GRATITUDE.

What were the highlights of your week?

GOOD DAYS START WITH

GRATITUDE

Develop an attitude of gratitude, and give thanks for everything that happens to you, knowing that every step forward is a step toward achieving something bigger and better than your current situation.

– Brian Tracy

I AM THANKFUL FOR...   DATE:

1. _____
2. _____
3. _____

I AM THANKFUL FOR...   DATE:

1. _____
2. _____
3. _____

I AM THANKFUL FOR...   DATE:

1. _____
2. _____
3. _____

I AM THANKFUL FOR...   DATE:

1. _____
2. _____
3. _____

I AM THANKFUL FOR...   DATE:

1. _____
2. _____
3. _____

I AM THANKFUL FOR...   DATE:

1. _____
2. _____
3. _____

I AM THANKFUL FOR...   DATE:

1. _____
2. _____
3. _____

CULTIVATE AN ATTITUDE OF GRATITUDE.

What were the highlights of your week?

GOOD DAYS START WITH

GRATITUDE

The discipline of gratitude is the explicit effort
to acknowledge that all I am and have is given
to me as a gift of love, a gift to be celebrated
with joy.

– Henri Nouwen

I AM THANKFUL FOR...   DATE:

1.

2.

3.

I AM THANKFUL FOR...   DATE:

1.

2.

3.

I AM THANKFUL FOR...   DATE:

1.

2.

3.

I AM THANKFUL FOR...   DATE:
....

1. _____
2. _____
3. _____

I AM THANKFUL FOR...   DATE:
....

1. _____
2. _____
3. _____

I AM THANKFUL FOR...   DATE:
....

1. _____
2. _____
3. _____

I AM THANKFUL FOR...   DATE:
....

1. _____
2. _____
3. _____

• •

CULTIVATE AN ATTITUDE OF GRATITUDE.

What were the highlights of your week?

• •

....

begin
each day
with a
grateful
heart

....

Write about one person that you are truly grateful for knowing.

_____

_____

_____

_____

_____

_____

_____

_____

_____

_____

_____

_____

_____

_____

_____

_____

_____

_____

_____

_____

_____

GRATITUDE

Enjoy the little things, for one day you may look back and realize they were the big things.

- Robert Brault

I AM THANKFUL FOR...   DATE:

1. _____
2. _____
3. _____

I AM THANKFUL FOR...   DATE:

1. _____
2. _____
3. _____

I AM THANKFUL FOR...   DATE:

1. _____
2. _____
3. _____

I AM THANKFUL FOR...   DATE:

1. _____

2. _____

3. _____

I AM THANKFUL FOR...   DATE:

1. _____

2. _____

3. _____

I AM THANKFUL FOR...   DATE:

1. _____

2. _____

3. _____

I AM THANKFUL FOR...   DATE:

1. _____

2. _____

3. _____

CULTIVATE AN ATTITUDE OF GRATITUDE.

What were the highlights of your week?

GOOD DAYS START WITH

GRATITUDE

When I started counting my blessings, my
whole life turned around.

– Willie Nelson

I AM THANKFUL FOR...   DATE:

1. _____
2. _____
3. _____

I AM THANKFUL FOR...   DATE:

1. _____
2. _____
3. _____

I AM THANKFUL FOR...   DATE:

1. _____
2. _____
3. _____

I AM THANKFUL FOR...   DATE:
....

1. _____
2. _____
3. _____

I AM THANKFUL FOR...   DATE:
....

1. _____
2. _____
3. _____

I AM THANKFUL FOR...   DATE:
....

1. _____
2. _____
3. _____

I AM THANKFUL FOR...   DATE:
....

1. _____
2. _____
3. _____

• •

CULTIVATE AN ATTITUDE OF GRATITUDE.

What were the highlights of your week?

• •

GOOD DAYS START WITH

GRATITUDE

Gratitude makes sense of our past, brings peace for today, and creates a vision for tomorrow.

– Melody Beattie

I AM THANKFUL FOR...   DATE:

1. _____
2. _____
3. _____

I AM THANKFUL FOR...   DATE:

1. _____
2. _____
3. _____

I AM THANKFUL FOR...   DATE:

1. _____
2. _____
3. _____

I AM THANKFUL FOR...   DATE:

1. _____
2. _____
3. _____

I AM THANKFUL FOR...   DATE:

1. _____
2. _____
3. _____

I AM THANKFUL FOR...   DATE:

1. _____
2. _____
3. _____

I AM THANKFUL FOR...   DATE:

1. _____
2. _____
3. _____

CULTIVATE AN ATTITUDE OF GRATITUDE.

What were the highlights of your week?

GOOD DAYS START WITH

GRATITUDE

> I always find beauty in things that are odd and imperfect – they are much more interesting.
>
> *– Marc Jacobs*

I AM THANKFUL FOR...   DATE:

1. _____
2. _____
3. _____

I AM THANKFUL FOR...   DATE:

1. _____
2. _____
3. _____

I AM THANKFUL FOR...   DATE:

1. _____
2. _____
3. _____

I AM THANKFUL FOR...   DATE:
· ·

1.
2.
3.

I AM THANKFUL FOR...   DATE:
· ·

1.
2.
3.

I AM THANKFUL FOR...   DATE:
· ·

1.
2.
3.

I AM THANKFUL FOR...   DATE:
· ·

1.
2.
3.

• •

CULTIVATE AN ATTITUDE OF GRATITUDE.

What were the highlights of your week?

• •

GOOD DAYS START WITH

GRATITUDE

He is a wise man who does not grieve for the things which he has not, but rejoices for those which he has.

- Epictetus

I AM THANKFUL FOR...   DATE:

1. _____

2. _____

3. _____

I AM THANKFUL FOR...   DATE:

1. _____

2. _____

3. _____

I AM THANKFUL FOR...   DATE:

1. _____

2. _____

3. _____

I AM THANKFUL FOR...   DATE:
. . . .

1. _____
2. _____
3. _____

I AM THANKFUL FOR...   DATE:
. . . .

1. _____
2. _____
3. _____

I AM THANKFUL FOR...   DATE:
. . . .

1. _____
2. _____
3. _____

I AM THANKFUL FOR...   DATE:
. . . .

1. _____
2. _____
3. _____

• •

CULTIVATE AN ATTITUDE OF GRATITUDE.

What were the highlights of your week?

• •

GOOD DAYS START WITH

GRATITUDE

In ordinary life, we hardly realize that we receive a great deal more than we give, and that it is only with gratitude that life becomes rich.

– Dietrich Bonhoeffer

I AM THANKFUL FOR...   DATE:

1. _____
2. _____
3. _____

I AM THANKFUL FOR...   DATE:

1. _____
2. _____
3. _____

I AM THANKFUL FOR...   DATE:

1. _____
2. _____
3. _____

I AM THANKFUL FOR...   DATE:
....

1. _____
2. _____
3. _____

I AM THANKFUL FOR...   DATE:
....

1. _____
2. _____
3. _____

I AM THANKFUL FOR...   DATE:
....

1. _____
2. _____
3. _____

I AM THANKFUL FOR...   DATE:
....

1. _____
2. _____
3. _____

· ·

CULTIVATE AN ATTITUDE OF GRATITUDE.

What were the highlights of your week?

· ·

GOOD DAYS START WITH

GRATITUDE

When we focus on our gratitude, the tide of disappointment goes out and the tide of love rushes in.

- Kristin Armstrong

I AM THANKFUL FOR...   DATE:

1. _____
2. _____
3. _____

I AM THANKFUL FOR...   DATE:

1. _____
2. _____
3. _____

I AM THANKFUL FOR...   DATE:

1. _____
2. _____
3. _____

I AM THANKFUL FOR...   DATE:
. . . .

1. _____
2. _____
3. _____

I AM THANKFUL FOR...   DATE:
. . . .

1. _____
2. _____
3. _____

I AM THANKFUL FOR...   DATE:
. . . .

1. _____
2. _____
3. _____

I AM THANKFUL FOR...   DATE:
. . . .

1. _____
2. _____
3. _____

• •

CULTIVATE AN ATTITUDE OF GRATITUDE.

What were the highlights of your week?

• •

GOOD DAYS START WITH

GRATITUDE

Have kindness, empathy, and gratitude every single day.

- Jennifer Aniston

I AM THANKFUL FOR...   DATE:

1. _____
2. _____
3. _____

I AM THANKFUL FOR...   DATE:

1. _____
2. _____
3. _____

I AM THANKFUL FOR...   DATE:

1. _____
2. _____
3. _____

I AM THANKFUL FOR...   DATE:
....

1. _____
2. _____
3. _____

I AM THANKFUL FOR...   DATE:
....

1. _____
2. _____
3. _____

I AM THANKFUL FOR...   DATE:
....

1. _____
2. _____
3. _____

I AM THANKFUL FOR...   DATE:
....

1. _____
2. _____
3. _____

• •

CULTIVATE AN ATTITUDE OF GRATITUDE.

What were the highlights of your week?

• •

GOOD DAYS START WITH

GRATITUDE

God gave us the gift of life; it is up to us to give ourselves the gift of living well.

– Voltaire

I AM THANKFUL FOR...   DATE:

1. _____
2. _____
3. _____

I AM THANKFUL FOR...   DATE:

1. _____
2. _____
3. _____

I AM THANKFUL FOR...   DATE:

1. _____
2. _____
3. _____

I AM THANKFUL FOR...   DATE:
....

1. _____
2. _____
3. _____

I AM THANKFUL FOR...   DATE:
....

1. _____
2. _____
3. _____

I AM THANKFUL FOR...   DATE:
....

1. _____
2. _____
3. _____

I AM THANKFUL FOR...   DATE:
....

1. _____
2. _____
3. _____

• •

CULTIVATE AN ATTITUDE OF GRATITUDE.

What were the highlights of your week?

• •

GOOD DAYS START WITH

GRATITUDE

We should certainly count our blessings, but
we should also make our blessings count.

– Neal A. Maxwell

I AM THANKFUL FOR...   DATE:

1. _____
2. _____
3. _____

I AM THANKFUL FOR...   DATE:

1. _____
2. _____
3. _____

I AM THANKFUL FOR...   DATE:

1. _____
2. _____
3. _____

I AM THANKFUL FOR...   DATE:

1. _____
2. _____
3. _____

I AM THANKFUL FOR...   DATE:

1. _____
2. _____
3. _____

I AM THANKFUL FOR...   DATE:

1. _____
2. _____
3. _____

I AM THANKFUL FOR...   DATE:

1. _____
2. _____
3. _____

CULTIVATE AN ATTITUDE OF GRATITUDE.

What were the highlights of your week?

GOOD DAYS START WITH

GRATITUDE

This a wonderful day. I've never seen this one before.

- Maya Angelou

I AM THANKFUL FOR...   DATE:
....

1._____
2._____
3._____

I AM THANKFUL FOR...   DATE:
....

1._____
2._____
3._____

I AM THANKFUL FOR...   DATE:
....

1._____
2._____
3._____

I AM THANKFUL FOR...   DATE:

1.
2.
3.

I AM THANKFUL FOR...   DATE:

1.
2.
3.

I AM THANKFUL FOR...   DATE:

1.
2.
3.

I AM THANKFUL FOR...   DATE:

1.
2.
3.

CULTIVATE AN ATTITUDE OF GRATITUDE.

What were the highlights of your week?

count
your
blessings

Write about one experience that you are grateful for that shaped who you are today.

_____

_____

_____

_____

_____

_____

_____

_____

_____

_____

_____

_____

_____

_____

_____

_____

_____

_____

_____

_____

_____

_____

GRATITUDE

When you are grateful - when you can see what you have - you unlock blessings to flow in your life.

- Suze Orman

I AM THANKFUL FOR...   DATE:

1. _____
2. _____
3. _____

I AM THANKFUL FOR...   DATE:

1. _____
2. _____
3. _____

I AM THANKFUL FOR...   DATE:

1. _____
2. _____
3. _____

I AM THANKFUL FOR...   DATE:
....

1. _____

2. _____

3. _____

I AM THANKFUL FOR...   DATE:
....

1. _____

2. _____

3. _____

I AM THANKFUL FOR...   DATE:
....

1. _____

2. _____

3. _____

I AM THANKFUL FOR...   DATE:
....

1. _____

2. _____

3. _____

• •

CULTIVATE AN ATTITUDE OF GRATITUDE.

What were the highlights of your week?

• •

GOOD DAYS START WITH

GRATITUDE

The true secret of happiness lies in taking a
genuine interest in all the details of daily life.

- William Morris

I AM THANKFUL FOR...   DATE:

1. _____
2. _____
3. _____

I AM THANKFUL FOR...   DATE:

1. _____
2. _____
3. _____

I AM THANKFUL FOR...   DATE:

1. _____
2. _____
3. _____

I AM THANKFUL FOR...   DATE:
....

1. _____
2. _____
3. _____

I AM THANKFUL FOR...   DATE:
....

1. _____
2. _____
3. _____

I AM THANKFUL FOR...   DATE:
....

1. _____
2. _____
3. _____

I AM THANKFUL FOR...   DATE:
....

1. _____
2. _____
3. _____

• ••

CULTIVATE AN ATTITUDE OF GRATITUDE.

What were the highlights of your week?

• ••

GOOD DAYS START WITH

GRATITUDE

> Some old fashioned things like fresh air and
> sunshine are hard to beat.
>
> *– Laura Ingalls Wilder*

I AM THANKFUL FOR...   DATE:

1. _____
2. _____
3. _____

I AM THANKFUL FOR...   DATE:

1. _____
2. _____
3. _____

I AM THANKFUL FOR...   DATE:

1. _____
2. _____
3. _____

I AM THANKFUL FOR...   DATE:

1. _____
2. _____
3. _____

I AM THANKFUL FOR...   DATE:

1. _____
2. _____
3. _____

I AM THANKFUL FOR...   DATE:

1. _____
2. _____
3. _____

I AM THANKFUL FOR...   DATE:

1. _____
2. _____
3. _____

CULTIVATE AN ATTITUDE OF GRATITUDE.

What were the highlights of your week?

GOOD DAYS START WITH

GRATITUDE

Blessed are they who see beautiful things
in humble places where other people see
nothing.

– Camille Pissarro

I AM THANKFUL FOR...   DATE:

1. _____

2. _____

3. _____

I AM THANKFUL FOR...   DATE:

1. _____

2. _____

3. _____

I AM THANKFUL FOR...   DATE:

1. _____

2. _____

3. _____

I AM THANKFUL FOR...   DATE:

1. _____
2. _____
3. _____

I AM THANKFUL FOR...   DATE:

1. _____
2. _____
3. _____

I AM THANKFUL FOR...   DATE:

1. _____
2. _____
3. _____

I AM THANKFUL FOR...   DATE:

1. _____
2. _____
3. _____

CULTIVATE AN ATTITUDE OF GRATITUDE.

What were the highlights of your week?

GOOD DAYS START WITH

GRATITUDE

The most important thing is to enjoy your life -
to be happy - it's all that matters.

- Audrey Hepburn

I AM THANKFUL FOR...   DATE:

1. _____
2. _____
3. _____

I AM THANKFUL FOR...   DATE:

1. _____
2. _____
3. _____

I AM THANKFUL FOR...   DATE:

1. _____
2. _____
3. _____

I AM THANKFUL FOR...   DATE:

1. _____

2. _____

3. _____

I AM THANKFUL FOR...   DATE:

1. _____

2. _____

3. _____

I AM THANKFUL FOR...   DATE:

1. _____

2. _____

3. _____

I AM THANKFUL FOR...   DATE:

1. _____

2. _____

3. _____

CULTIVATE AN ATTITUDE OF GRATITUDE.

What were the highlights of your week?

GOOD DAYS START WITH

GRATITUDE

Acknowledging the good that you already have in your life is the foundation for all abundance.

– Eckhart Tolle

I AM THANKFUL FOR...   DATE:

1. _____
2. _____
3. _____

I AM THANKFUL FOR...   DATE:

1. _____
2. _____
3. _____

I AM THANKFUL FOR...   DATE:

1. _____
2. _____
3. _____

I AM THANKFUL FOR...   DATE:

1. _____

2. _____

3. _____

I AM THANKFUL FOR...   DATE:

1. _____

2. _____

3. _____

I AM THANKFUL FOR...   DATE:

1. _____

2. _____

3. _____

I AM THANKFUL FOR...   DATE:

1. _____

2. _____

3. _____

CULTIVATE AN ATTITUDE OF GRATITUDE.

What were the highlights of your week?

GOOD DAYS START WITH

GRATITUDE

Sometimes we should express our gratitude
for the small and simple things like the scent of
the rain, the taste of your favorite food, or the
sound of a loved one's voice.

– Joseph B. Worthlin

I AM THANKFUL FOR...   DATE:

1. _____
2. _____
3. _____

I AM THANKFUL FOR...   DATE:

1. _____
2. _____
3. _____

I AM THANKFUL FOR...   DATE:

1. _____
2. _____
3. _____

I AM THANKFUL FOR...   DATE:
....

1. _____
2. _____
3. _____

I AM THANKFUL FOR...   DATE:
....

1. _____
2. _____
3. _____

I AM THANKFUL FOR...   DATE:
....

1. _____
2. _____
3. _____

I AM THANKFUL FOR...   DATE:
....

1. _____
2. _____
3. _____

• •

CULTIVATE AN ATTITUDE OF GRATITUDE.

What were the highlights of your week?

• •

GOOD DAYS START WITH

GRATITUDE

I am happy because I'm grateful. I choose to be grateful. That gratitude allows me to be happy.

- Will Arnett

I AM THANKFUL FOR...   DATE:
....

1. _____
2. _____
3. _____

I AM THANKFUL FOR...   DATE:
....

1. _____
2. _____
3. _____

I AM THANKFUL FOR...   DATE:
....

1. _____
2. _____
3. _____

I AM THANKFUL FOR...   DATE:

1. _____
2. _____
3. _____

I AM THANKFUL FOR...   DATE:

1. _____
2. _____
3. _____

I AM THANKFUL FOR...   DATE:

1. _____
2. _____
3. _____

I AM THANKFUL FOR...   DATE:

1. _____
2. _____
3. _____

CULTIVATE AN ATTITUDE OF GRATITUDE.

What were the highlights of your week?

GRATITUDE

> Put your heart, mind, and soul into even your
> smallest acts. This is the secret of success.
>
> *- Swami Sivananda*

I AM THANKFUL FOR...   DATE:

1. _____
2. _____
3. _____

I AM THANKFUL FOR...   DATE:

1. _____
2. _____
3. _____

I AM THANKFUL FOR...   DATE:

1. _____
2. _____
3. _____

I AM THANKFUL FOR...   DATE:

1. _____
2. _____
3. _____

I AM THANKFUL FOR...   DATE:

1. _____
2. _____
3. _____

I AM THANKFUL FOR...   DATE:

1. _____
2. _____
3. _____

I AM THANKFUL FOR...   DATE:

1. _____
2. _____
3. _____

CULTIVATE AN ATTITUDE OF GRATITUDE.

What were the highlights of your week?

GOOD DAYS START WITH

GRATITUDE

Gratitude helps you to grow and expand;
gratitude brings joy and laughter into your life
and into the lives of all those around you.

– Eileen Caddy

I AM THANKFUL FOR...   DATE:

1. _____
2. _____
3. _____

I AM THANKFUL FOR...   DATE:

1. _____
2. _____
3. _____

I AM THANKFUL FOR...   DATE:

1. _____
2. _____
3. _____

I AM THANKFUL FOR...   DATE:

1. _____
2. _____
3. _____

I AM THANKFUL FOR...   DATE:

1. _____
2. _____
3. _____

I AM THANKFUL FOR...   DATE:

1. _____
2. _____
3. _____

I AM THANKFUL FOR...   DATE:

1. _____
2. _____
3. _____

CULTIVATE AN ATTITUDE OF GRATITUDE.

What were the highlights of your week?

....

today
i am
grateful

....

Write about one place you are thankful that you had
the opportunity to visit and why.

_____

_____

_____

_____

_____

_____

_____

_____

_____

_____

_____

_____

_____

_____

_____

_____

_____

_____

_____

_____

_____

_____

GOOD DAYS START WITH

GRATITUDE

Be thankful for what you have; you'll end up having more. If you concentrate on what you don't have, you will never, ever have enough.

– Oprah Winfrey

I AM THANKFUL FOR...   DATE:

1. _____
2. _____
3. _____

I AM THANKFUL FOR...   DATE:

1. _____
2. _____
3. _____

I AM THANKFUL FOR...   DATE:

1. _____
2. _____
3. _____

I AM THANKFUL FOR...   DATE:

1.
2.
3.

I AM THANKFUL FOR...   DATE:

1.
2.
3.

I AM THANKFUL FOR...   DATE:

1.
2.
3.

I AM THANKFUL FOR...   DATE:

1.
2.
3.

CULTIVATE AN ATTITUDE OF GRATITUDE.

What were the highlights of your week?

GOOD DAYS START WITH

GRATITUDE

If you are gracious, you have won the game.
- Stevie Nicks

I AM THANKFUL FOR...   DATE:

1. _____
2. _____
3. _____

I AM THANKFUL FOR...   DATE:

1. _____
2. _____
3. _____

I AM THANKFUL FOR...   DATE:

1. _____
2. _____
3. _____

I AM THANKFUL FOR...   DATE:

1. _____

2. _____

3. _____

I AM THANKFUL FOR...   DATE:

1. _____

2. _____

3. _____

I AM THANKFUL FOR...   DATE:

1. _____

2. _____

3. _____

I AM THANKFUL FOR...   DATE:

1. _____

2. _____

3. _____

CULTIVATE AN ATTITUDE OF GRATITUDE.

What were the highlights of your week?

GOOD DAYS START WITH

GRATITUDE

I like canceled plans. And empty bookstores.
I like rainy days and thunderstorms. And quiet
coffee shops. I like messy beds and over-worn
pajamas. Most of all, I like the small joys that a
simple life brings.

– *Unknown*

I AM THANKFUL FOR...   DATE:

1. _____
2. _____
3. _____

I AM THANKFUL FOR...   DATE:

1. _____
2. _____
3. _____

I AM THANKFUL FOR...   DATE:

1. _____
2. _____
3. _____

I AM THANKFUL FOR...   DATE:

1. _____

2. _____

3. _____

I AM THANKFUL FOR...   DATE:

1. _____

2. _____

3. _____

I AM THANKFUL FOR...   DATE:

1. _____

2. _____

3. _____

I AM THANKFUL FOR...   DATE:

1. _____

2. _____

3. _____

CULTIVATE AN ATTITUDE OF GRATITUDE.

What were the highlights of your week?

GOOD DAYS START WITH

GRATITUDE

That art of being happy lies in the power of
extracting happiness from common things.

– Henry Ward Beecher

I AM THANKFUL FOR...   DATE:

1. _____
2. _____
3. _____

I AM THANKFUL FOR...   DATE:

1. _____
2. _____
3. _____

I AM THANKFUL FOR...   DATE:

1. _____
2. _____
3. _____

I AM THANKFUL FOR...   DATE:
. . . .

1. _____
2. _____
3. _____

I AM THANKFUL FOR...   DATE:
. . . .

1. _____
2. _____
3. _____

I AM THANKFUL FOR...   DATE:
. . . .

1. _____
2. _____
3. _____

I AM THANKFUL FOR...   DATE:
. . . .

1. _____
2. _____
3. _____

• •

CULTIVATE AN ATTITUDE OF GRATITUDE.

What were the highlights of your week?

• •

GRATITUDE

> The real gift of gratitude is that the more grateful you are, the more present you become.
>
> – *Robert Holden*

I AM THANKFUL FOR...   DATE:

1. _____
2. _____
3. _____

I AM THANKFUL FOR...   DATE:

1. _____
2. _____
3. _____

I AM THANKFUL FOR...   DATE:

1. _____
2. _____
3. _____

I AM THANKFUL FOR...   DATE:
....

1. _____
2. _____
3. _____

I AM THANKFUL FOR...   DATE:
....

1. _____
2. _____
3. _____

I AM THANKFUL FOR...   DATE:
....

1. _____
2. _____
3. _____

I AM THANKFUL FOR...   DATE:
....

1. _____
2. _____
3. _____

• •

CULTIVATE AN ATTITUDE OF GRATITUDE.
What were the highlights of your week?

• •

GRATITUDE

> Gratitude and attitude are not challenges; they are choices.
>
> – *Robert Braathe*

I AM THANKFUL FOR...   DATE:

1. _____
2. _____
3. _____

I AM THANKFUL FOR...   DATE:

1. _____
2. _____
3. _____

I AM THANKFUL FOR...   DATE:

1. _____
2. _____
3. _____

I AM THANKFUL FOR...   DATE:

1.
2.
3.

I AM THANKFUL FOR...   DATE:

1.
2.
3.

I AM THANKFUL FOR...   DATE:

1.
2.
3.

I AM THANKFUL FOR...   DATE:

1.
2.
3.

CULTIVATE AN ATTITUDE OF GRATITUDE.

What were the highlights of your week?

GOOD DAYS START WITH

GRATITUDE

In life, one has a choice to take one of two paths: to wait for some special day--or to celebrate each special day.

- Rasheed Ogunlaru

I AM THANKFUL FOR...   DATE:

1. _____
2. _____
3. _____

I AM THANKFUL FOR...   DATE:

1. _____
2. _____
3. _____

I AM THANKFUL FOR...   DATE:

1. _____
2. _____
3. _____

I AM THANKFUL FOR...   DATE:

1. _____
2. _____
3. _____

I AM THANKFUL FOR...   DATE:

1. _____
2. _____
3. _____

I AM THANKFUL FOR...   DATE:

1. _____
2. _____
3. _____

I AM THANKFUL FOR...   DATE:

1. _____
2. _____
3. _____

CULTIVATE AN ATTITUDE OF GRATITUDE.

What were the highlights of your week?

GOOD DAYS START WITH

GRATITUDE

Through the eyes of gratitude, everything is a
miracle.

- Mary Davis

I AM THANKFUL FOR...   DATE:

1. _____

2. _____

3. _____

I AM THANKFUL FOR...   DATE:

1. _____

2. _____

3. _____

I AM THANKFUL FOR...   DATE:

1. _____

2. _____

3. _____

I AM THANKFUL FOR...   DATE:
....

1. _____
2. _____
3. _____

I AM THANKFUL FOR...   DATE:
....

1. _____
2. _____
3. _____

I AM THANKFUL FOR...   DATE:
....

1. _____
2. _____
3. _____

I AM THANKFUL FOR...   DATE:
....

1. _____
2. _____
3. _____

• •

CULTIVATE AN ATTITUDE OF GRATITUDE.

What were the highlights of your week?

• •

GOOD DAYS START WITH

GRATITUDE

Sometimes the smallest things take up the most room in your heart.

– Winnie the Pooh

I AM THANKFUL FOR...   DATE:
. . . .

1. _____

2. _____

3. _____

I AM THANKFUL FOR...   DATE:
. . . .

1. _____

2. _____

3. _____

I AM THANKFUL FOR...   DATE:
. . . .

1. _____

2. _____

3. _____

I AM THANKFUL FOR...   DATE:

1. _____
2. _____
3. _____

I AM THANKFUL FOR...   DATE:

1. _____
2. _____
3. _____

I AM THANKFUL FOR...   DATE:

1. _____
2. _____
3. _____

I AM THANKFUL FOR...   DATE:

1. _____
2. _____
3. _____

CULTIVATE AN ATTITUDE OF GRATITUDE.

What were the highlights of your week?

GOOD DAYS START WITH

GRATITUDE

Happiness is not something you postpone for the future; it is something you design for the present.

– *Jim Rohn*

I AM THANKFUL FOR...   DATE:

1. _____

2. _____

3. _____

I AM THANKFUL FOR...   DATE:

1. _____

2. _____

3. _____

I AM THANKFUL FOR...   DATE:

1. _____

2. _____

3. _____

I AM THANKFUL FOR...   DATE:

1. _____
2. _____
3. _____

I AM THANKFUL FOR...   DATE:

1. _____
2. _____
3. _____

I AM THANKFUL FOR...   DATE:

1. _____
2. _____
3. _____

I AM THANKFUL FOR...   DATE:

1. _____
2. _____
3. _____

CULTIVATE AN ATTITUDE OF GRATITUDE.

What were the highlights of your week?

GOOD DAYS START WITH

GRATITUDE

Gratitude can transform common days into
thanksgivings, turn routine jobs into joy, and
change ordinary opportunities into blessings.

– William Arthur Ward

I AM THANKFUL FOR...   DATE:

1. _____
2. _____
3. _____

I AM THANKFUL FOR...   DATE:

1. _____
2. _____
3. _____

I AM THANKFUL FOR...   DATE:

1. _____
2. _____
3. _____

I AM THANKFUL FOR...   DATE:

1. _____
2. _____
3. _____

I AM THANKFUL FOR...   DATE:

1. _____
2. _____
3. _____

I AM THANKFUL FOR...   DATE:

1. _____
2. _____
3. _____

I AM THANKFUL FOR...   DATE:

1. _____
2. _____
3. _____

CULTIVATE AN ATTITUDE OF GRATITUDE.

What were the highlights of your week?

give
thanks

Write about some of the ways that you can show your gratitude to others.

_____

_____

_____

_____

_____

_____

_____

_____

_____

_____

_____

_____

_____

_____

_____

_____

_____

_____

_____

_____

_____

_____

_____

GOOD DAYS START WITH

GRATITUDE

The most simple things can bring the most happiness.

- Izabella Scorupco

I AM THANKFUL FOR...   DATE:

1. _____
2. _____
3. _____

I AM THANKFUL FOR...   DATE:

1. _____
2. _____
3. _____

I AM THANKFUL FOR...   DATE:

1. _____
2. _____
3. _____

I AM THANKFUL FOR...   DATE:

1. _____
2. _____
3. _____

I AM THANKFUL FOR...   DATE:

1. _____
2. _____
3. _____

I AM THANKFUL FOR...   DATE:

1. _____
2. _____
3. _____

I AM THANKFUL FOR...   DATE:

1. _____
2. _____
3. _____

CULTIVATE AN ATTITUDE OF GRATITUDE.

What were the highlights of your week?

GOOD DAYS START WITH

GRATITUDE

Very little is needed to make a happy life; it is all within yourself, in your way of thinking.

- Marcus Aurelius

I AM THANKFUL FOR...   DATE:

1. _____
2. _____
3. _____

I AM THANKFUL FOR...   DATE:

1. _____
2. _____
3. _____

I AM THANKFUL FOR...   DATE:

1. _____
2. _____
3. _____

I AM THANKFUL FOR...   DATE:
....

1. _____
2. _____
3. _____

I AM THANKFUL FOR...   DATE:
....

1. _____
2. _____
3. _____

I AM THANKFUL FOR...   DATE:
....

1. _____
2. _____
3. _____

I AM THANKFUL FOR...   DATE:
....

1. _____
2. _____
3. _____

• •

CULTIVATE AN ATTITUDE OF GRATITUDE.

What were the highlights of your week?

• •

GOOD DAYS START WITH

GRATITUDE

> If you want to turn your life around, try thankful-ness. It will change your life mightily.
>
> *- Gerald Good*

I AM THANKFUL FOR...　　　DATE:

1. _____
2. _____
3. _____

I AM THANKFUL FOR...　　　DATE:

1. _____
2. _____
3. _____

I AM THANKFUL FOR...　　　DATE:

1. _____
2. _____
3. _____

I AM THANKFUL FOR...   DATE:
....

1. _____
2. _____
3. _____

I AM THANKFUL FOR...   DATE:
....

1. _____
2. _____
3. _____

I AM THANKFUL FOR...   DATE:
....

1. _____
2. _____
3. _____

I AM THANKFUL FOR...   DATE:
....

1. _____
2. _____
3. _____

• •

CULTIVATE AN ATTITUDE OF GRATITUDE.

What were the highlights of your week?

• •

GOOD DAYS START WITH

GRATITUDE

> Gratitude unlocks the fullness of life. It turns what we have into enough, and more. It turns denial into acceptance, chaos to order, confusion to clarity. It can turn a meal into a feast, a house into a home, a stranger into a friend.
>
> *– Melody Beattie*

I AM THANKFUL FOR...   DATE:

1. _____
2. _____
3. _____

I AM THANKFUL FOR...   DATE:

1. _____
2. _____
3. _____

I AM THANKFUL FOR...   DATE:

1. _____
2. _____
3. _____

I AM THANKFUL FOR...   DATE:

1. _____
2. _____
3. _____

I AM THANKFUL FOR...   DATE:

1. _____
2. _____
3. _____

I AM THANKFUL FOR...   DATE:

1. _____
2. _____
3. _____

I AM THANKFUL FOR...   DATE:

1. _____
2. _____
3. _____

CULTIVATE AN ATTITUDE OF GRATITUDE.

What were the highlights of your week?

GOOD DAYS START WITH

GRATITUDE

Things turn out best for people who make the
best of the way things turn out.

— *John Wooden*

I AM THANKFUL FOR...   DATE:

1. _____
2. _____
3. _____

I AM THANKFUL FOR...   DATE:

1. _____
2. _____
3. _____

I AM THANKFUL FOR...   DATE:

1. _____
2. _____
3. _____

I AM THANKFUL FOR...   DATE:
....

1. _____
2. _____
3. _____

I AM THANKFUL FOR...   DATE:
....

1. _____
2. _____
3. _____

I AM THANKFUL FOR...   DATE:
....

1. _____
2. _____
3. _____

I AM THANKFUL FOR...   DATE:
....

1. _____
2. _____
3. _____

• •

CULTIVATE AN ATTITUDE OF GRATITUDE.

What were the highlights of your week?

• •

GOOD DAYS START WITH

GRATITUDE

I am determined to be cheerful and happy in whatever situation I may find myself. For I have learned that the greater part of our misery or un-happiness is determined not by our circumstance but by our disposition.

– Martha Washington

I AM THANKFUL FOR...   DATE:

1. _____
2. _____
3. _____

I AM THANKFUL FOR...   DATE:

1. _____
2. _____
3. _____

I AM THANKFUL FOR...   DATE:

1. _____
2. _____
3. _____

I AM THANKFUL FOR...   DATE:

1. _____
2. _____
3. _____

I AM THANKFUL FOR...   DATE:

1. _____
2. _____
3. _____

I AM THANKFUL FOR...   DATE:

1. _____
2. _____
3. _____

I AM THANKFUL FOR...   DATE:

1. _____
2. _____
3. _____

CULTIVATE AN ATTITUDE OF GRATITUDE.

What were the highlights of your week?

GOOD DAYS START WITH

GRATITUDE

Start where you are. Use what you have. Do what you can.

- Aurther Ashe

I AM THANKFUL FOR...   DATE:

1. _____
2. _____
3. _____

I AM THANKFUL FOR...   DATE:

1. _____
2. _____
3. _____

I AM THANKFUL FOR...   DATE:

1. _____
2. _____
3. _____

I AM THANKFUL FOR...   DATE:
. . . .

1._____

2._____

3._____

I AM THANKFUL FOR...   DATE:
. . . .

1._____

2._____

3._____

I AM THANKFUL FOR...   DATE:
. . . .

1._____

2._____

3._____

I AM THANKFUL FOR...   DATE:
. . . .

1._____

2._____

3._____

• •

CULTIVATE AN ATTITUDE OF GRATITUDE.

What were the highlights of your week?

• •

GOOD DAYS START WITH

GRATITUDE

If you want to find happiness, find gratitude.

- Steve Maraboli

I AM THANKFUL FOR...   DATE:

1. _____
2. _____
3. _____

I AM THANKFUL FOR...   DATE:

1. _____
2. _____
3. _____

I AM THANKFUL FOR...   DATE:

1. _____
2. _____
3. _____

I AM THANKFUL FOR...   DATE:

1. _____

2. _____

3. _____

I AM THANKFUL FOR...   DATE:

1. _____

2. _____

3. _____

I AM THANKFUL FOR...   DATE:

1. _____

2. _____

3. _____

I AM THANKFUL FOR...   DATE:

1. _____

2. _____

3. _____

CULTIVATE AN ATTITUDE OF GRATITUDE.

What were the highlights of your week?

GOOD DAYS START WITH

GRATITUDE

Trade your expectation for appreciation and
the world changes instantly.

- Tony Robbins

I AM THANKFUL FOR...   DATE:

1. _____
2. _____
3. _____

I AM THANKFUL FOR...   DATE:

1. _____
2. _____
3. _____

I AM THANKFUL FOR...   DATE:

1. _____
2. _____
3. _____

I AM THANKFUL FOR...   DATE:
· ·

1. _____
2. _____
3. _____

I AM THANKFUL FOR...   DATE:
· ·

1. _____
2. _____
3. _____

I AM THANKFUL FOR...   DATE:
· ·

1. _____
2. _____
3. _____

I AM THANKFUL FOR...   DATE:
· ·

1. _____
2. _____
3. _____

· ·

CULTIVATE AN ATTITUDE OF GRATITUDE.

What were the highlights of your week?

· ·

GOOD DAYS START WITH

GRATITUDE

It is the sweet, simple things of life which are the real ones after all.

- Laura Ingalls Wilder

I AM THANKFUL FOR...   DATE:

1. _____

2. _____

3. _____

I AM THANKFUL FOR...   DATE:

1. _____

2. _____

3. _____

I AM THANKFUL FOR...   DATE:

1. _____

2. _____

3. _____

I AM THANKFUL FOR...   DATE:
. . . .

1. _____
2. _____
3. _____

I AM THANKFUL FOR...   DATE:
. . . .

1. _____
2. _____
3. _____

I AM THANKFUL FOR...   DATE:
. . . .

1. _____
2. _____
3. _____

I AM THANKFUL FOR...   DATE:
. . . .

1. _____
2. _____
3. _____

• •

CULTIVATE AN ATTITUDE OF GRATITUDE.

What were the highlights of your week?

• •

....

good
days
start
with
gratitude

....

Reflect on how journaling 3 things you are thankful for everyday has changed your life.

_____

_____

_____

_____

_____

_____

_____

_____

_____

_____

_____

_____

_____

_____

_____

_____

_____

_____

_____

_____

_____

_____

_____

_____

. . . .

Visit our website

www.prettysimplebooks.com

And find us on Instagram

@prettysimplebooks

. . . .

We love connecting with you!